The Union Soldier

by Renée C. Rebman

Content Adviser: Brett Barker, Ph.D.
Assistant Professor, Department of History,
University of Wisconsin–Marathon County

Reading Adviser: Rosemary G. Palmer, Ph. D.
Department of Literacy, College of Education,
Boise State University

COMPASS POINT BOOKS
MINNEAPOLIS, MINNESOTA

Compass Point Books
3109 West 50th Street, #115
Minneapolis, MN 55410

Visit Compass Point Books on the Internet at *www.compasspointbooks.com*
or e-mail your request to *custserv@compasspointbooks.com*

On the cover: Ten Union officers posed in front of building at Acquia Creek, February, 1863.

Photographs ©: Library of Congress, cover, 10, 11, 13, 18, 33, 34, back cover; Prints Old and Rare, back cover (far left); Stock Montage/Getty Images, 4; North Wind Picture Archives, 5, 26; Bettmann/Corbis, 6, 20, 39, 40; Corbis, 8, 9, 14, 16, 19, 21, 24, 25, 36, 37; Medford Historical Society Collection/Corbis, 12, 23; The Granger collection, New York, 15, 22; Museum of the City of New York/Corbis, 17; Image courtesy of Robert Hunt Rhodes and Gregg A. Mierka, 27; Wisconsin Historical Society/WHi-38951, 28; DVIC/NARA, 29; Abraham Lincoln Presidential Library, 31; State Archives of Michigan, 32; Louie Psihoyos/Corbis, 38; Ric Ergenbright/Corbis, 41.

Editor: Shelly Lyons
Page Production: Blue Tricycle
Photo Researcher: Abbey Fitzgerald
Cartographer: XNR Productions, Inc.
Library Consultant: Kathleen Baxter

Creative Director: Keith Griffin
Editorial Director: Carol Jones
Managing Editor: Catherine Neitge

For my mother, Joan Zajack *RR*

Library of Congress Cataloging-in-Publication Data
Rebman, Renée C., 1961–
  The Union soldier / by Renée C. Rebman.
    p. cm.—(We the people)
  Includes bibliographical references and index.
  ISBN-13: 978-0-7565-2030-4 (hardcover)
  ISBN-10: 0-7565-2030-4 (hardcover)
  ISBN-13: 978-0-7565-2042-7 (paperback)
  ISBN-10: 0-7565-2042-8 (paperback)
  1. United States. Army—History—Civil War, 1861–1865—Juvenile literature. 2. United States. Army—Military life—History—19th century—Juvenile literature. 3. Soldiers—United States—History—19th century—Juvenile literature. 4. United States—History—Civil War,
1861–1865—Equipment and supplies—Juvenile literature. I. Title. II. We the people (Series)
(Compass Point Books)
  E492.R43 2007
  973.7'41—dc22   2006003944

TABLE OF CONTENTS

PUTTING DOWN THE SOUTHERN REBELLION

On April 15, 1861, Abraham Lincoln, the president of the United States, asked for 75,000 male volunteers for the Union Army to "put down the Southern rebellion." He was preparing for war against the Confederate States of America. Men were asked to serve for 90 days. In Northern cities, streets filled with citizens waving the American flag, and eager young men rushed to enlist in the Army.

More than half of the volunteers were farmers or farmers' sons. Some were recent immigrants who came from countries such as

Abraham Lincoln

4

Military volunteers parade through the streets as soldiers prepared for the Civil War.

Ireland, Germany, and Norway. Many of the men had
never traveled outside of their home states. Joining the
Army presented an opportunity for adventure and glory.

The spirit of patriotism was strong. Restoring the
Union was of primary importance to them, because the
Union represented the freedoms and opportunities that
their society was used to and proud of. One New York City
man wrote, "The feeling runs mountains high, and thousands

5

The Civil War tore apart the nation and produced numerous brutal conflicts.

of men are offering their services where hundreds only
are required."

Tension between the North and South over the issue
of slavery had been mounting for years. Soon after

Abraham Lincoln was elected president in 1860, South Carolina seceded, or broke away from, the Union. Six more states followed— Mississippi, Florida, Alabama, Georgia, Louisiana, and Texas. The seven states formed the Confederate States of America. They named Jefferson Davis as their president.

Confederate President Jefferson Davis

The country had been divided, and the main differences centered around slavery and states' rights. Some Northerners believed that slavery should be abolished, but most simply wanted to keep slavery from spreading to new territories. Wealthy Southerners relied on slave labor in order to make money on their plantations, and they wanted to preserve their states' rights to keep slavery legal. They also wanted the right to allow slavery to spread.

7

Confederate troops attacked Fort Sumter in an attempt to take the fort from the Union.

On April 12, 1861, the Confederate militia fired upon Union troops at Fort Sumter in Charleston, South Carolina. Three days later, Lincoln put out the call for more troops. Soon, Virginia, Arkansas, Tennessee, and North Carolina also joined the Confederacy. The Civil War was just beginning.

IN TRAINING

In 1860, one year before the Civil War began, the United States Army had about 16,000 men. By 1865, close to 2 million men had joined during the course of the war. Most of the men who enlisted were untrained and had never experienced battle.

Soldiers trained to serve in infantry, cavalry, or artillery units. The infantry was made up of foot soldiers. Most of the soldiers who served in the war were in the infantry. The cavalry soldiers rode on horseback. They scouted the

A Union soldier with his gear

9

Union artillerymen stood next to their cannon.

enemy's position and rode their horses into battle. Horses pulled the heavy cannons to the battle site. Artillerymen trained to load, aim, and shoot the powerful cannons with speed and accuracy.

At the beginning of the war, there weren't enough weapons for the Union soldiers to take into battle. President Lincoln admitted, "The plain matter of fact is, our good people have rushed to the rescue of the govern-

New York State militiamen near Harper's Ferry, Virginia, in 1861

ment, faster than the government can find arms to put into their hands."

Some men began training with old-fashioned muskets. Lucky soldiers received a Springfield rifle, which had a longer range and better accuracy. Learning to load and shoot a weapon properly could mean life or death. Each time the gun was fired, a cartridge containing the ball and

11

Company C, 110th Pennsylvania Infantry Regiment at Falmouth, Virginia

gunpowder had to be loaded into it. During the heat of battle, a mistake could cause the gun to misfire or not fire at all.

Later in the war, some Union soldiers received repeating rifles. These guns could fire many rapid shots without being reloaded. One soldier's journal reported, "I think the Johnny's (Confederate soldiers) are getting rattled; they are afraid of our repeating rifles. They say we are not fair, that we have guns that we load up on Sunday and shoot all the rest of the week. This I know, I feel a good deal more confidence in myself with a 16 shooter in my hands than I used to with a single shot rifle."

One of the Union's best assets was its artillery. Men and horses traveled in small groups known as batteries. Four to six horses pulled the big guns. More horses pulled the caissons, the carts that carried ammunition and supplies. The Union's

Artillerymen and cavalrymen used horses in battle.

Union officers stood next to a large cannon.

powerful cannons shot heavy cannonballs at the Confederate soldiers. Howitzers and mortars were smaller than
cannons and fired shells and exploding ammunition at
the enemy.

Soldiers soon learned that marching and drilling, or
handling their guns, would take up most of their day. One

14

soldier wrote, "The first thing in the morning is drill, then drill, then drill again. Then drill, drill, a little more drill. Then drill and lastly drill. Between drills, we drill and sometimes stop to eat a little and have a roll call."

Weeks and months of training made the new soldiers eager to try their skills in battle. A soldier in the 72nd

13-inch (33-centimeter) mortar at Petersburg, Virginia, in 1864

15

Illinois Infantry wrote, "Men want to be tried to see what they are made of." Another from the 2nd Rhode Island Regiment said, "We are all impatient to get into Virginia and have a brush with the rebels."

Union soldiers in camp at Harper's Ferry, Virginia, in 1862

Approximately 850 soldiers were killed in the first Battle of Bull Run in July 1861.

They soon got their chance. On July 21, 1861, the first Battle of Bull Run was fought near Manassas Junction, Virginia. The Union soldiers were finally fighting a battle— or "seeing the elephant," as they called it. The first battle of Bull Run proved to be a devastating defeat for the Union Army, and it marked the beginning of four long years of tough battles.

CAMP LIFE

Officers, cooks, and nurses bustled around soldiers' camps. In some cases, wives and family members of officers huddled around campfires outside their small tents. Known as camp followers, they pitched in to help provide food or care for the sick or wounded. But most wives and

18

Women and children at a Union military camp in 1861

family members remained at home, so soldiers often felt lonely.

Food provided by the Army was scarce and often spoiled or riddled with maggots. The hungry soldiers enjoyed it when the sutler's wagon rolled around. Sutlers followed Union camps and sold goods to the soldiers. They offered cheese, butter, sardines, and personal supplies such

A sutler's tent advertised oysters for sale in 1862.

as writing paper. A soldier paid 50 cents for 1 pound (.45 kilogram) of cheese and $1 for 1 pound (.45 kg) of butter. These prices were very expensive for that time.

When food was scarce, soldiers survived on hardtack. These giant crackers were 3 inches (7.6 cm) across and ½ inch (1.3 cm) thick and were made of flour and water. Soldiers called the crackers "worm castles" because they were often infested with weevils. Frying worm castles in grease killed the weevils, and soldiers called this treat skillygalee. Soldiers would often soak hardtack in coffee to soften the hard crackers.

Camp life could be boring, and soldiers tried to entertain themselves with music and games. Sometimes Union camps were so close to Confederate camps that the soldiers sang to each other.

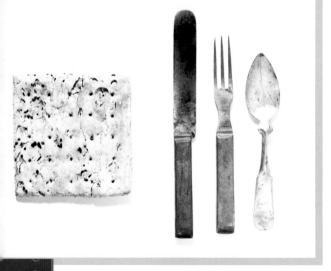

A Union soldier's mess kit items included hardtack.

Games like baseball helped pass the soldiers' time. Competitions were a popular pastime as well. Seeing who could catch a greased pig, shoot at a target, or run the fastest kept the men occupied.

Soldiers often played musical instruments to pass the time in camp.

21

Soldiers also played cards and read books and newspapers. They read letters from home over and over again. One Union soldier confided in his diary, "We have received no mail for several days and do not like it. A soldier can do without hard bread but not without his letters from home."

One of the worst problems soldiers faced was disease. Many people lived close together in unsanitary conditions.

A man with a cart sold newspapers to soldiers in camp.

Camp tents were pitched close together.

Disease spread quickly and killed more men than enemy attacks. Historians disagree on the exact number, but some say that nearly 224,000 Union soldiers died from disease during the war, while 110,000 died in battle.

"Camp fever," another name for typhoid fever, killed thousands of soldiers. Malaria, pneumonia, dysentery, and smallpox also spread through camps. Diarrhea could become so severe it was fatal.

Women of the U.S. Sanitary Commission helped improve hospital conditions.

To improve conditions in the camps, Northern women formed the United States Sanitary Commission (USSC). This group collected food, mattresses, warm clothing, and bandages for soldiers. The USSC also raised money for supplies and helped move wounded soldiers to homes where they could recover.

24

SOLDIERS AND LEADERS

The fighting on the battlefields spread across several miles. Large cannons boomed and gun shells flashed. Smoke from gunshots filled the air. Soldiers, half-blind in the smoky haze, advanced on the enemy and fired shot after shot. Some men mistakenly killed their own troops.

Strong leadership was important to the Union's successes on the battlefields. In February 1862, Union General Ulysses S. Grant gained control of Fort Donelson in Tennessee. The Confederate commander realized he could not win the fight and asked Grant to make an agreement with

Union General Ulysses S. Grant

25

him. Grant replied, "No terms except an unconditional and immediate surrender can be accepted." Grant led his troops to many more victories, including Vicksburg and Chattanooga. In March 1864, President Lincoln promoted him to general-in-chief of the Union Army. Grant's military strategy helped him defeat General Robert E. Lee in 1865 and bring an end to the war.

Union General William Tecumseh Sherman

Another strong Union leader was General William Tecumseh Sherman, whose troops destroyed farms, buildings, and other property on their quest to capture Atlanta, Georgia, in September 1864. Two months later, he marched his troops across Georgia all the way to the Atlantic Ocean. They hoped the destruction would weaken the Confederates' morale. Sherman's army was unstoppable. His troops' famous March to the Sea, as it came to be called, showed Confederates that their own army could not protect them.

Leaders like Sherman and Grant worked together with their soldiers to win the war. Even under the worst battlefield conditions, they refused to quit.

Elisha Hunt Rhodes of Rhode Island was only 19 years old when he enlisted as a soldier with the 2nd Regiment of Rhode Island Volunteer Infantry. He kept a diary during the war, which was later published as *All for the Union: The Civil War Diary and Letters of Elisha Hunt Rhodes.* When describing the soldiers' anticipation of battle, he wrote, "Tomorrow I

Elisha Hunt Rhodes wrote a Civil War diary. **27**

Rufus Dawes was 19 years old when he joined the Union Army.

suppose we shall try and shoot a few rebels. I wish it was over for it is worse for a soldier to wait for a battle to begin than it is to do the fighting."

Rufus Dawes, of the 6th Wisconsin Volunteer Infantry, also wrote about his Civil War experiences in his book, *Service with the Sixth Wisconsin Volunteers.* In one letter, he wrote about the Battle of Gettysburg, the bloodiest battle of the war: "The Sixth has lost so far one hundred and sixty men. Since the first day we have lost only six. O, Mary, it is sad to look at our shattered band of devoted men. Only four field officers in the brigade have escaped and I am one of them."

Union soldiers like Rhodes and Dawes left a legacy

28

through their written words. They have helped generations of Americans understand exactly what Civil War soldiers went through and for what they were fighting.

No one anticipated the war would last four years. Because each battle took many lives, the Union needed more soldiers. As the war continued, the U.S. government offered volunteers a bounty, or bonus, of $300 to join or

Recruiting took place in the New York City Hall Park in 1864.

29

re-enlist. That was more money than most men made in a whole year. This caused a problem known as bounty jumping. Men would enlist, take the money, and then desert. Some would enlist again somewhere else to get more money.

Another issue was the enlistment process, in which medical exams were not very thorough. Women disguised as men were sometimes able to join the Army, but this was a rare occurrence. These women were radical for their time, since most women were expected to remain at home.

Jennie Hodgers enlisted in 1862 as Albert Cashier. She served with the 95th Illinois Infantry for the next three years. During a bloody battle at Vicksburg, Mississippi, Confederate forces captured Hodgers. Fearless and determined to rejoin her regiment, Hodgers seized a guard's gun, knocked the man down, and fled back to the Union camp.

After the war, Hodgers continued to live as a man, using the name Cashier. Her sex was discovered when she was admitted to a state hospital in 1911. Upon her death at

Woman Soldier in 95th Ill.

ALBERT D. J. CASHIER

ALBERT D. J. CASHIER

Jennie Hodgers disguised herself as Albert D.J. Cashier.

the age of 68, she was given a military funeral, even though many of her friends knew she was a woman. Her tombstone reads: "Albert D.J. Cashier, Co. 6, 95 Ill. Inf."

Sarah Emma Edmonds was also determined to serve her country. She joined the Union Army using the name

Sarah Emma Edmonds disguised herself as Frank Thompson and joined the Army.

Frank Thompson. She served as a spy, soldier, and male nurse. As a spy, Edmonds was sent on various missions. She disguised herself as an Irish peddler woman and as a black laundress. Her first chance at combat came with the First Battle of Bull Run in July 1861. She was present at other battles, too.

Despite the volunteers who enlisted, the U.S. Congress passed a draft law in February 1863. If volunteer numbers were low, men were chosen at random and required to enlist. Although the majority of Union soldiers were volunteers, a wealthy man who was drafted sometimes avoided serving by paying another man to take his place. These purchased soldiers were often poor men who

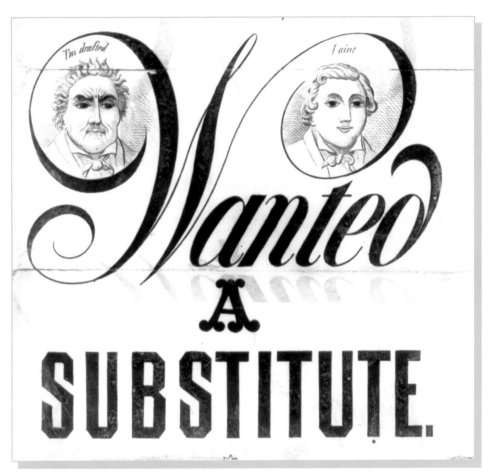

The Enrollment Act of 1863 allowed drafted men to purchase a substitute.

needed the money for their family's survival. Also, until 1864, drafted men were allowed to pay a $300 commutation fee to avoid serving.

At first, the soldiers were eager to fight and expected the war to end quickly. But the Union suffered many

33

In New York City, blindfolded men drew names for the draft in 1863.

defeats, and the soldiers became discouraged. However, the Union soldiers kept fighting because they were committed to the Union's cause.

34

AFRICAN-AMERICAN TROOPS

Even though slavery had been banned in the North, government leaders were reluctant to let African-Americans join the Army. The U.S. secretary of war issued a statement declaring, "This Department has no intention at the present to call into service of the government any colored soldiers."

On August 6, 1861, the U.S. government declared that slaves in the Confederate Army would be confiscated by the Union Army. The Union government planned to employ these men as cooks, laborers, and caretakers of wounded Union soldiers.

Slaves by the thousands escaped to the North. Many homeless slaves lived in camps together. Many of them wanted to fight for the Union rather than simply work. They formed their own regiments and asked for the right to enlist, but Congress was slow to accept their help.

35

A group of freed slaves worked with the 13th Massachusetts Infantry Regiment.

Finally, in July 1862, Congress passed a bill that allowed free blacks to enlist in the Union Army. The Bureau of Colored Troops was formed to organize African-American regiments.

Frederick Douglass, a former slave and famed abolitionist, recruited African-Americans for military service. In his monthly newsletter, he wrote an article challenging black men to join the Union Army. Through his efforts, Douglass helped recruit more than 100 free blacks, including two of his own sons.

However, African-American troops did not have the same support from the government as white soldiers. They were given sub-standard rations and supplies, and their pay scale was lower.

Frederick Douglass was a spokesperson for African-Americans.

A white soldier earned $13 per month, but a black soldier earned only $10. In many cases, the medical treatment black soldiers received was also inferior. Some doctors did not even want to treat black soldiers.

White officers were required to lead African-American regiments, but some white officers refused this duty. In addition, some Union soldiers were reluctant to

37

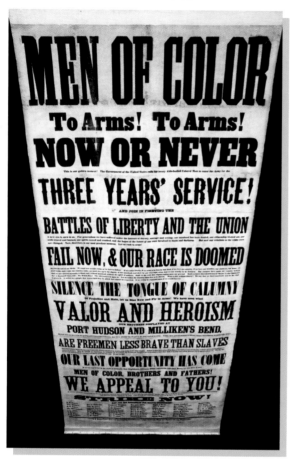

A recruitment sign called for African-Americans to join the Army.

fight alongside black troops because they falsely believed them to be poor soldiers. Those feelings often changed as African-Americans proved their worth on the battlefield.

One of the most famous black regiments was the 54th Massachusetts Regiment, which was led by Colonel Robert Gould Shaw. In July 1863, the 54th faced intense fighting at the Battle of Fort Wagner on Morris Island, South Carolina. Shaw ordered his men to "take the fort or die there." Outnumbered nearly three to one by Confederates, Shaw's men charged the fort.

The men of the 54th Regiment fell quickly.

When Confederate troops shot the soldier holding the Union flag, Union Sergeant William H. Carney grabbed the flag and carried it high, determined to deliver it safely back to the regiment. Union soldiers were ordered to retreat. Bullets flew, and Carney was shot in the head, arm, chest, and leg, but he made it back to camp with the flag.

Colonel Robert Gould Shaw led the 54th Massachusetts Regiment

The 54th lost half of its men in the battle, including Colonel Shaw. The Confederate troops buried him in a mass grave with his soldiers. Stories of the battle spread throughout the Union Army. The regiment had proved its bravery. Sergeant Carney was given the Congressional Medal of Honor for his courage. He was the first African-

American to receive this honor.

Approximately 120,000 African-American soldiers fought in the Civil War. About 38,000 of them died in service, but most died of disease. Hundreds stayed in the Army after the war ended. Serving in peacetime regiments, they helped settle the West.

Most Union soldiers fought bravely to keep the Union together. These soldiers faced horrible living conditions, disease, and brutal battles for four long years.

The 54th Massachusetts Regiment fought bravely at Fort Wagner.

A monument at the Gettysburg National Cemetery in Pennsylvania

Many lost their lives. Others returned home to rebuild
their lives. But all are remembered and honored for their
bravery, dedication, and service.

GLOSSARY

abolished—ended

abolitionist—person who supported the banning of slavery

Confederate States of America—the Southern states that fought against the Northern states in the Civil War; also called the Confederacy

draft—a system that chooses people who are compelled by law to serve in the military

drilling—exercising or training soldiers in marching and in executing movements with a weapon

enlist—to join the armed services

militia—military force, often made up of volunteers

regiment—a military group made up of about 1,000 soldiers

seceded—withdrew from a group

Union—the United States of America; also the Northern states that fought against the Southern states in the Civil War

weevil—a type of beetle that is destructive to nuts, fruit, grain, and plants

DID YOU KNOW?

- Union soldiers' uniforms were blue and made of wool. The wool was extremely warm, especially in hot weather, but it was very durable. Soldiers also wore a blue wool cap called a kepi.

- Confederate President Jefferson Davis fled Richmond, Virginia, shortly before Union troops captured the city on April 2, 1865. He was later apprehended by the U.S. government and served two years in prison for treason.

- The great abolitionist Harriet Tubman served as a spy for the Union, reporting the movements of Confederate troops. She also helped many slaves to freedom on the Underground Railroad.

IMPORTANT DATES

Timeline

1860	In November, Abraham Lincoln is elected president of the United States; in December, South Carolina secedes from the Union.
1861	In April, Confederate troops fire on Fort Sumter; President Lincoln asks for volunteers for the Union Army.
1862	In September, Congress rules that free African-Americans can enlist in the Union Army.
1863	In January, President Lincoln issues the Emancipation Proclamation; in March, the Union begins drafting soldiers.
1864	In September, General Sherman captures the city of Atlanta, Georgia; in November, Lincoln is elected to a second term; Sherman's troops capture Savannah, Georgia, after their March to the Sea.
1865	In April, Confederate General Robert E. Lee surrenders to Union General Ulysses S. Grant at Appomattox Court House, Virginia; Abraham Lincoln is assassinated.

IMPORTANT PEOPLE

JEFFERSON DAVIS (1808–1889)

Senator from Mississippi from 1847 to 1861; President of the Confederate States of America from 1861 to 1865

FREDERICK DOUGLASS (1817–1895)

A former slave and famous abolitionist who later became a well-known author and speaker; recruited African-American men for the Union Army

ULYSSES S. GRANT (1822–1885)

General of the Union Army who accepted Confederate General Robert E. Lee's surrender in 1865; President of the United States for two terms, from 1869 to 1877

ABRAHAM LINCOLN (1809–1865)

President of the United States from 1861 to 1865; signed the Emancipation Proclamation in 1863; assassinated by a Confederate sympathizer in 1865

WILLIAM T. SHERMAN (1820–1891)

General of the Union Army from 1862 to 1865; led his troops on a March to the Sea from Atlanta to Savannah, Georgia

WANT TO KNOW MORE?

At the Library

Day, Nancy. *Your Travel Guide to Civil War America.* Minneapolis:
Runestone Press, 2001.

Dunn, John, ed. *Union Soldiers: Voices from the Civil War.* San Diego:
Blackbirch Press, 2003.

Ford, Carin T. *African-American Soldiers in the Civil War: Fighting for
Freedom.* Berkeley Heights, N.J.: Enslow Publishers, 2004.

On the Web

For more information on the *Union Soldier,* use FactHound
to track down Web sites related to this book.

1. Go to *www.facthound.com*

2. Type this book ID: 0756520304

3. Click on the *Fetch It* button.

Your trusty FactHound will fetch the best Web sites for you!

46

On the Road

Gettysburg National Military Park

97 Taneytown Road

Gettysburg, PA 17325

Markers, monuments, and a cemetery on the famous battlefield

The National Civil War Museum

One Lincoln Circle

Reservoir Park

Harrisburg, PA 17103

Equally balanced presentation of the Union and Confederate sides of the Civil War

Look for more We the People books about this era:

The Assassination of Abraham Lincoln
ISBN 0-7565-0678-6

Battle of the Ironclads
ISBN 0-7565-1628-5

The Carpetbaggers
ISBN 0-7565-0834-7

The Confederate Soldier
ISBN 0-7565-2025-8

The Dred Scott Decision
ISBN 0-7565-2026-6

The Emancipation Proclamation
ISBN 0-7565-0209-8

Fort Sumter
ISBN 0-7565-1629-3

The Gettysburg Address
ISBN 0-7565-1271-9

Great Women of the Civil War
ISBN 0-7565-0839-8

The Lincoln-Douglas Debates
ISBN 0-7565-1632-3

The Missouri Compromise
ISBN 0-7565-1634-X

The Reconstruction Amendments
ISBN 0-7565-1636-6

Surrender at Appomattox
ISBN 0-7565-1626-9

The Underground Railroad
ISBN 0-7565-0102-4

Women of the Confederacy
ISBN 0-7565-2033-9

Women of the Union
ISBN 0-7565-2035-5

A complete list of We the People titles is available on our Web site:
www.compasspointbooks.com

INDEX

About the Author

Renée C. Rebman lives in Lexington, Ohio. She has written several nonfiction books for children and particularly enjoys historical subjects. She is also a published playwright. Her plays are produced in schools and community theaters across the country.